GROW YOUR WEALTH

HOW TO
GENERATE
REAL ESTATE
LEADS ONLINE

TUCKER FERWERDA

Grow Your Wealth

How To Generate Real Estate Leads Online

Tucker Ferwerda

Grow Your Wealth: How To Generate Real Estate Leads Online

Copyright © 2020 by Tucker Ferwerda

Dedication

I dedicate this book to my wife, Kara, my two kids Bobbie and Owen, and to my friends, family, and mentors who have helped me become who I am today.

I'd also like to dedicate this book to you, the reader, on your many future successes that you will get after finishing this book. I look forward to seeing your posts and deals as you grow your real estate business online.

As an added bonus, I'd like to do something very special for you. Head over to www.digitalrealestateexperts.com to watch a BONUS free training on how you can start generating real estate leads online.

Table of Contents

Preface

I would like to acknowledge a few people in my book. I would like to first acknowledge, my Father in heaven who has blessed me so much with everything that He has given me up until this point, all of my skills, all of my abilities, and my acquired talents as well as my God-given talents. I'm grateful for all of the things that I've been given in my journey to become that better person that He wants me to be.

I also want to acknowledge my mom and dad for raising me with such a strong work ethic. Without them, I don't know where I'd be. I've learned a lot of things from them as well as what to do and what not to do. And really, my Father in heaven and my parents have made me what I am today.

Secondly, I'd like to thank my friends and family who provide daily support along my journey, who've always been positive, who've always pushed me to fulfill my dreams. It's just been amazing to have that level of support from everybody. I want to thank my team. I want to thank all of my past sucky jobs. I want to thank every single person that has come into my existence that has helped me progress forward.

I'm very grateful for every person, including the few haters and enemies because sometimes it happens. I'm thankful for all of those factors lining up to culminate into who I am today so that through this book, I can help you, the reader.

This book is dedicated and written for those people who are focused and results-driven, who are professionals, influencers, coaches, and companies in the real estate niche. I ensure that this book provides meticulous tactics that will allow you to grow your real estate business.

This book is not for whiners, complainers, weak, timid couch potatoes who are lazy, not for people who are closed-minded, or for people who are rude, self-centered, not for people who are arrogant, or ignorant, not for people who are selfish, greedy, dishonest, unreliable, hypocritical, fake, the kind of people who give sob story after sob story and are small-minded. This book is not meant for people who have a negative outlook on life and act accordingly.

This book is only for people who are positive and optimistic, who want to achieve the best results possible, who will bend over backward to help someone in need. This book is for driven professionals, influencers, coaches, and companies in the real estate niche.

The purpose of the book is to help real estate professionals drive more business to their company through social media and digital marketing. It's also meant to drive more quality leads. It's intended to give your company more exposure and a long-lasting legacy of producing high-quality products and services.

Once you've read this book, you will know precisely how to leverage digital marketing to lay the foundations of your business as well as to grow your business into an empire. I realize that's a sweeping statement, but I get very specific with my five-step process, the Prelaunch Profit Method, that you'll employ to get results.

Our focus is on how to grow your business through education and personal branding. We're going to be learning how to create a personal brand around yourself online to get more deals, get more coaching students, and to crush it online by producing more leads, closing more deals, and living the life that you've always dreamed of.

You are in good hands and have chosen the right book written by the right person because this book is not written from theory. This is actually coming from real-time data that I'm collecting on a regular basis. The best way for you to succeed is to make a routine of documenting and producing content so that you can make tons of money.

Now, you may have some objections already, and I've heard them all: You don't have enough time. You're not tech-savvy. You don't have the right team or enough money. You don't want to use social media. You don't need to create a personal brand. Maybe you don't want to coach, or you don't want more coaching students to get more deals. You might not know where to start or how it works.

People often wonder why should I fix it if nothing is broken? Or that they will never be able to learn everything about digital marketing to get results. Lots of folks have no desire to learn digital marketing or social media.

Others think branding, sales funnels, and follow-up systems are unnecessary. They're comfortable where they are, so why change? Who needs to be the next Grant Cardone?

Whatever your excuse or objection, it's okay. I totally get where you're coming from. You are about to discover why and how digital marketing of your real estate business will generate more leads, close more deals, and grow your income as well as your legacy.

Whether you want to grow through more leads, secure more properties, close more deals, become a real estate coach, speaker, or consultant, creating a personal brand inside of your current real estate business will educate people on *how* and *why* they should do business with you.

I'm going to take you step-by-step on how to grow your real estate business online so that you can start adapting to the trends in the market.

Introduction

You are in good hands and have chosen the right book written by the right person because this book is not written from theory. This is actually coming from real-time data that I'm collecting on a regular basis. Here are just a few of the things we've been able to do in a few short years:

- We've surveyed over 4000 real estate professionals and have a database of all their answers of their major pain points and struggles over the past 3 years
- We've helped real estate companies and professionals generate thousands of leads with free and paid forms of advertising, which in return have produced hundreds of thousands of dollars.
- We help real estate professionals launch their businesses online, everything from lead generation for more deals or to help them sell more courses, coaching packages, events, and books.
- We help real estate professionals become #1 in their industry, market, and niche.

The best way for you to succeed in real estate today is by leveraging digital marketing and social media platforms to create a personal brand around your real estate business. I'll show you why inside of this book.

Chapter One: 6-7 Figures Per Month

There are significant gaps, as we speak, between the real estate world, social media, and digital marketing. By the time you've finished this book—and it's not long—you'll walk away with a comprehensive and actionable understanding of how to grow your real estate business online. In fact, you'll conduct exercises throughout the book that will yield results before you get to the last page. You'll have a thorough and practical understanding of how to grow your real estate business online, by touching more people, producing more leads, and closing more deals to finally realize the lifestyle you've been working so hard for.

I'm no stranger to manual labor. When I was younger, I lived the drudgery of working in warehouses and construction. I despised it. I woke up at five every morning with an angry gnawing in my stomach that stayed with me as I physically exhausted myself at the warehouses and construction sites. I just didn't mesh with people there; they didn't get me. I felt like an outsider with my passion for personal development, my drive to make serious money, and my thirst for learning. That's when I experienced the bitter taste of a soul-sucking grind and the loneliness of being surrounded by folks—nice as they were—who didn't share the same vibe.

The day-in and day-out repetition pulverized my brain to mush. I had to get out. I felt the same way about college; I hated learning 60-year-old information from 60-year-olds who taught me something that was either obsolete now or would be within that next year. I had to do something about it. A change had to happen.

Podcasts were an escape and a lifeline as I tossed boxes of Cheetos and Fritos into the back of a 53-foot semi-truck. Voices of optimism, hope, and know-how streamed into my soul and offered a lifeline when I was drowning in a life I was never meant to live.

I remember the salty aroma that came from the boxes filled with chips, the smell of diesel, the bloodshot eyes of my coworkers, and how thirsty I was in the very moment I had my life-changing breakthrough. I was listening to a podcast episode that, in a very practical way, presented the idea that not only could you make six and seven figures per year, but that you could actually make six and seven figures per month from *digital marketing*! Digital marketing. And digital marketing could achieve those same results with any given business.

Now we've come full circle to that gap I talked about earlier in the digital real estate space. That means whether you are a real estate agent, a real estate coach, a real estate investor, a mortgage loan officer, a remodeler, a contractor, or even a custom home builder, there is a mammoth need for digital marketing in your industry. By the time you finish reading this book, you will have a firm foundation and understanding of digital marketing through the Prelaunch Profit Method.

This book is short because it's meant to be read in its entirety. I'm about to share with you the same five steps I employ in my digital marketing strategies that get results for any type of business. The Prelaunch Profit Method grows a company from ground-zero to ground-hero through digital marketing and online advertising. You will avoid hiring the wrong people, going down the wrong road, and becoming overwhelmed as you seek to create better offers, generate more leads, and close more deals. I know that dialing in the Prelaunch Profit Method will grow your business online and scale it to the moon because it works.

The most significant struggle I've witnessed in my clients is their *mindset.* People grapple with understanding how technology and social media work. They get frustrated with their systems. Some folks have shiny-object syndrome, where they bounce from product to product or advertising platform to advertising platform. You may be trying to find the right people to put inside of your business. Just about everybody has had the challenge of employing the right processes *and* the right people. You may not have the right framework and not even know it. Maybe you don't know what to do. What's the right platform, and when should you post?

Who do you trust? You may be struggling with spending too much money on things that don't work. Branding might be a challenge for you. Are you generating fewer leads than you want to on a regular basis? When it comes to social media, your head spins with sales funnels and techno mumbo-jumbo. Maybe you're having a hard time with research. You might be struggling with Facebook ads or Google ads or email marketing or hiring or firing or outsourcing. What about organic traffic, automation, and lead gen? No matter your challenge, no matter where you are, this book will lay the foundation to overcome your challenges and start to grow your real estate business.

I've had clients who experienced so much frustration and hated what they were doing, that they'd be overwhelmed with anxiety just hopping on the computer. Watching everyone around you succeed while you're left behind in the dust could leave you feeling confused and helpless. You may feel stress, guilty, and even ashamed because you have to get things done *now* that you should have done years ago, but just you haven't done them yet. Maybe you're embarrassed about where you're *not* because you compare yourself to other people's online posts about their awesome lifestyle as a result of their success and results.

You may be scared, fearful of judgment from other people who are close to you. Are you working with the wrong people who make fun of you behind your back? Whatever it is, I am here for you, and my goal is to give you the motivation and the results that you need to grow your real estate business online with digital marketing.

This book is for real estate companies and real estate professionals who want to simply focus on getting more deals. This book is also for real estate companies, and professionals who want to get more students enrolled in their coaching programs, courses, events, and more. This book is for companies and professionals who want to get more course sales. This book is for those who are ready to educate their customers on how to buy houses from them. This book is intended to give you the exact framework to start getting more deals into your business every single month, like clockwork.

The biggest takeaway and empowerment that I want my readers to have from my book would be that they can do anything they want in life. There are no limits to what you can reach. Nothing is holding you back from impacting the world and making a difference. A possible misconception that you might have currently of why I wrote this book is that I have a secret agenda. You might be thinking that I am after to win it for myself and not help anybody. You might be thinking that this whole idea, for you to create a personal brand around yourself or to create an education business is a scam and that it can never happen or whatever. But I'm here to tell you that since you have purchased this book and invested in me, my whole goal now is to help you from page one to page done on growing your real estate business by educating and helping you close more deals and live the lifestyle that you want by implementing digital marketing and social media marketing into your business.

The reason I believe I was put on this earth was to impact and influence as many people as I can on the earth, and my goal is to bring happiness to as many people as I can. Reading my book and implementing all that's inside will give my readers the exact framework to get more deals and grow your business online by generating more deals and generating more leads on a monthly basis.

Chapter Two: The Prelaunch Profit Method

How I realized that you can make multiple six and seven figures more per year than you've been doing right now through digital marketing and social media.

So with your current business, whether you are just starting as a real estate professional, whether you are a beginner real estate agent, a beginner real estate investor, a beginner real estate coach, a beginner, or even intermediate to advanced real estate coach, or maybe you are a Fortune 500 real estate company, you can start generating more business by implementing more digital marketing and social media marketing strategies into your business every single month.

The Prelaunch Profit Method will help you understand how to lay the foundations so that you can generate more leads, get more deals, and grow your business without spending money on the wrong things and the wrong people, which lead to costly mistakes in your business.

Now, there's a significant need in the real estate world to leverage social media and digital marketing. A lot of real estate professionals are not using social media to grow their brand, generate more leads, generate more deals, and grow their business. A lot of people think that they have to employ old and outdated ways of marketing to get more deals when the old forms of marketing are not as fluent or as effective as they used to be.

More than ever, there's an opportunity to generate more deals and grow your business via putting the right information out in the world that will earn you credibility and trust, while educating your prospects and clients.

An important way for you to think about my discovery and apply it to your life and your situation is that digital marketing is the new frontier, and you know others who are using it successfully. You know that it's something you need to do already to share your message with the world. By educating people, they will know, like, and trust you a lot more and will do more deals with you.

You know you are leaving a ton of money on the table, and you know you are missing out on so much opportunity. You also understand that you aren't reaching enough people in the world, and you also know that you have a story to tell that will literally turn your life around. You know that there is a ton of money to be made for those who act fast. You also understand that there is a tribe of buyers out there waiting for you to help them. You also know that their story can influence a lot of people.

So let me tell you two stories about people who I've helped when it came down to growing their real estate business through personal branding and education.

Dan Zitofsky is a wonderful real estate investor, a real estate coach, and a best-selling author. I helped him achieve the best-selling author status after being in the real estate space for almost 30 years. Dan was 19 when he got kicked out of the house because he didn't want to go to college, and he had to start making money. He became a local police officer and a firefighter, but Dan wanted to escape. That's when he became a real estate investor.

Dan started investing. He started getting more deals, and he discovered that he made more money from his deals than he did at his jobs. So, he quit his jobs, started getting more deals, and he's now conducted over 2000 transactions. Dan's been able to help thousands of people learn, and all of this has happened because of digital marketing and social media. I've been able to help him scale to multiple six figures with his online training and his lead generation, and he's on track to hitting seven figures with his education business. He's also been able to make millions of dollars' worth of deals from his Facebook profile.

Dan is one of the best students I've ever had, and he's one of the best strategic partners that I've ever had when it comes down to doing what is needed at the right time, at the right place, with the right people, to grow his real estate company. He's one of the most humble guys I know, and it's because of this humility he's been able to learn and grow and adapt his business to then turn it into a fully functioning brand online so that he can impact more people, close more deals, and grow his real estate company through digital marketing.

Now, let me also tell you a story about Kimanzi Constable. Kimanzi Constable is a Fortune 500 consultant who travels to an average of 39 countries per year and teaches companies how to grow via digital marketing. He was using just a simple WordPress website and a Square account when I began to work with him.

When we first started working together, I told him that he should be using a sales funnel machine called ClickFunnels to start growing his business. It took him a while to understand the importance of it, and at first, he didn't want to do it, but after he saw the magnitude of potential that it could have on his business, he dove in headfirst.

And after working through tech, after teaching him some social media tactics in advertising and helping him create sales funnels that converted, he's been able to now have his first six-figure month, by educating people about how to do business with him. He's made millions of dollars because of digital marketing. He has implemented email marketing and sales funnels to generate leads to grow his business with a personal brand and educating people about how to do business with him.

Dan and Kimanzi have leveraged social media and digital marketing to create a personal brand on social media by educating people to be able to grow their real estate business online.

Think about all of the real estate experts you know about online. Who do you follow? Whose posts do you engage with? Whose videos do you watch? These guys understand the power of social media and digital marketing. They have been able to grow their real estate companies, not just by doing typical deals and standard marketing, google them, and you're likely to see their ads pop up. They have leveraged information to grow their real estate companies so that they can get paid not only through deals and investing in real estate, but also educating people, through courses, coaching, events, books, or consulting. They've created and shared content online that has attracted people to do business with them.

These real estate investors are leveraging social media and digital marketing to create multiple streams of income, which grows their business exponentially. *They have built a business that revolves around educating people on how to give them money.*

Can you see how important digital marketing is now? Dan and Kimanzi aren't just getting more leads; they have created a personal brand around their businesses so that they can continue to create the "know, like, and trust" factor inside of their businesses so that they can generate more deals, get more leads, and grow their business in the real estate world.

In today's climate, *this* is the most efficient and effective method of producing real growth in your real estate business. People's attention is online, on their mobile devices, and it's only going to continue that way. That is the way the world currently works. There is more money spent online than on traditional advertising. Hands-down, marketing online is the best way to get business.

You might consider pursuing other options to grow your real estate business that are more aligned with traditional marketing methods. Now, while some do work, and may even get you some results, digital marketing is where you can start growing your business and having a long-lasting effect in your real estate business.

Think about creating traditional mailers to advertise your business, and you send them out to everybody, knowing that 90% of them are going to go straight into the trash. People consider those mailers junk mail. You've literally set up a marketing scheme where people are throwing your money away.

Now, with digital marketing, let's just say you ran Facebook Ads or Google Ads. You can keep that data and those ads so that you can continue to retarget those people and send them more offers and send them more ways to work with you versus them, throwing it in the trash. The more you advertise online, the smarter it becomes, the less money you spend, and you make more money because you're able to hit way more people at such a low cost.

Billboards are way too expensive these days; radio ads don't work like they used to, print magazines, and all of the traditional methods of marketing are inarguably less effective and more expensive than digital marketing simply because there is more data to back up your advertising efforts.

The reason traditional marketing efforts no longer work is that people ignore them, they feel old-school, and as I mentioned, people's focus is online. For example, people are listening to podcasts instead of the radio. The bottom line is traditional marketing methods are dying off, and it's time for individuals and businesses who want success to pivot. Companies are going out of business because they didn't adapt to the market. Amazon came along and took note of the trends. Jeff Bezos went into growing his website with digital marketing, and now it's one of the biggest companies in the world because he adapted to the market.

If you don't adapt to the market and take the necessary steps to generate more business in your real estate company, you risk going out of business. That's what happened to Toys "R" Us and Sears, who are barely scraping by because they weren't agile enough to pivot and adapt when Amazon entered the market.

Another reason why people fail to grow their business online is because they don't listen to their audience. They don't create offers or do customer research, and they don't conduct market research to understand the needs of their current and future audience. These folks don't have the necessary data to apply to an effective digital marketing strategy.

Large companies have the money to spend on digital marketing, which generates the data to inform them about what does and doesn't work. Research these companies to learn what they are doing with their digital marketing, and how you can implement the same strategy to grow your company.

Gary Vaynerchuk talks about how "attention" is the new currency. It's a simple concept: You will make money when you offer your services where the most attention is spent. It's as simple as that.

How many times have you driven past a billboard and actually called the number on it? How many times have you called an ad? Or how many times have you dialed the number from a print magazine or a radio advertisement or a TV commercial? How many times have you actually called the number from this type of ad?

But I know for a fact that you see ads regularly when you're scrolling Google and Facebook and all of these other social media platforms. You see their advertisements and click on them every single day. *That* is the power of digital marketing. Your business should be where people are spending their time and attention.

Let me tell you about another person who has leveraged digital marketing and social media to grow her brand. Barbara Corcoran is a real estate professional and real estate coach who started and grew her real estate business. She has a ton of followers on social media, and she is building her personal brand online and affecting the masses with her message.

The Prelaunch Profit Method will help to grow your real estate business online, just like it did for Kimanzi Constable. He had already done the work, but just needed that last little bit of help. He was producing content regularly, he had already been getting sales, but he was not streamlining his business and getting more sales and actually making more money per person that came and bought his training and programs.

The amazing thing that happened was that, after Kimanzi took one of my education programs, he hit his first six-figure month this past month as of the writing of this book, and he's sure to hit seven figures in his business.

That's why I'm so happy to share a powerful process that is not merely a theory, but one that is proven to get results. Consider the experts that you follow on social media. They have leveraged digital marketing to grow their personal brand by educating and sharing information, to then be able to grow and get more deals, get more students, sell more books, and get more speaking engagements. That is how they've become a well-rounded and sought-after expert.

Let me tell you another story so that I can further illustrate why you must get on social media and market your business through digital marketing and why you should start doing this stuff right away. This story speaks to Gary Vaynerchuk's idea about how attention is the new currency. Wherever you can place your business in front of people that you want to reach, where they are spending their attention, that is where you will actually start making the most money.

I'm going to share something with you that is shocking about my discovery. Research is king. The more questions you can ask inside of your business, and the more questions you can ask your potential customers and clients, the more money you will make. Most companies do not listen to their audience. Most companies think they have an idea for what is needed in the market, so they guess and second-guess, and they do all of this work that their audience doesn't need.

The main reason why big companies like Target and Sears have struggled over the years and became bankrupt is that they did not adapt to their market. When you can adapt and listen to your audience and know the market trends, you can then start adapting and pivoting your business decisions to then adapt to the market to help you grow your real estate company, and point it in the right direction, so that you do not go out of business or go bankrupt like Target or Sears.

This is amazing because research will make you a ton of money. By using customer and competitor research—the first step in the Prelaunch Profit Method —you will understand what your current and future audiences are saying so that they can become your current audience and clients.

You can discover competitor information online so that you don't have to go and create something from scratch. You can simply model successful companies and adapt your message and marketing efforts similar to how they are doing their marketing, but just do it better than them. This method has enabled me to help companies make a ton of money.

Let me tell you about another expert who is also doing this. Look at Tony Robbins. I fist-bumped Tony Robbins at one of his events one time after he told us that all his companies combined had an annual revenue in the billions. He's not only a public speaker, but he also sells his coaching packages and courses, he invests in real estate, and much more.

Let me now reveal the five steps of the Prelaunch Profit Method. The first step is research. Research involves customer and competitor research. By researching what your current audience wants, desires, needs, and fears, by asking them simple questions, you can start to understand what they are thinking, how they are feeling, and what they want. By asking these questions, you will then be able to tailor your message to your audience, so that you know exactly how you need to speak to them so that they know that you sincerely care about how you can help them, and then you can sell them what they want.

The other part of the research is competitor research. Like I said before, you need to research what is already working in the market, even companies that are not in your niche. You need research on what other people are doing successfully because it works. There's no point in reinventing the wheel and starting from scratch. There is already a ton of work out there. You just need to adapt, to find out what these companies are doing, and do it better. Or, you need to find someone who is already doing this stuff and pay the experts to actually implement it in your business.

Let's talk about the second step. The second step is creating an offer. Now, an offer is something that you give in exchange for something else, whether it is information, or whether it is money. When creating an offer, you need to be able to create something of value, such as a guide, a downloadable PDF, a course, etc. You need to give something in exchange for something else. The more offers you can create, the more your real estate business will grow. You need to create offers that people want. To find out what they want, you need to conduct customer research and ask them questions, whether it's on social media, whether it is from past content that you or other people have created, and through your email list.

The third step is plugging that offer into a sales system. A sales system is the lead generator, or landing page, where you leverage sales funnels to generate more leads, generate more sales, and grow your real estate company. This also includes email marketing and chatbots.

Step four is getting traffic, both organic and paid. You need to make sure that you are leveraging all social media platforms and all types of paid traffic, depending on where your current customer is. Facebook ads, YouTube ads, and Google ads are where you want to start.

Step five is to scale. You need to be able to scale after all this is said and done. Scaling involves creating more offers in the following ways: outsourcing more, hiring more team members and documenting processes and systems. Automating your business as much as possible is key. You'll want to automate your sales systems, so that you can have the systems working for you, instead of you working for your systems.

Most people think they need perfection to succeed when, in reality, what they actually need is 1% daily work, every single day. Focus on becoming better just 1% every single day, and focus on growing your company according to how things are currently working in the market.

Let me tell you another story about a person who has already started to grow his real estate company by educating people. Ben Fredricks is the farthest thing away from being a guru. Ben has a lot of relationships with auction companies around the United States and sells his properties for dirt-cheap prices. At the time of writing this book, he is growing his real estate company by educating people on how to buy his properties. Ben puts his offers online and on social media and gets people interested in his offers, whether it's to buy his properties, to learn from him, having him as a speaker, buying his online courses, or hiring him for coaching. He is not perfect, but he's started to lay down the foundation so that he can continue to grow his company by educating people about what he has to offer.

So, as you can see, it's not just gurus. Anyone can do this. I'm not a guru, and I started from the ground up doing this stuff, and I've helped companies generate hundreds of thousands of dollars through digital marketing, and it's only because of the Prelaunch Profit Method.

Chapter Three: The Perfect Posting System

One of the common roadblocks that you might be experiencing is being apprehensive about technology. Dan Zitofsky spent tens of thousands of dollars on the wrong people in his business. They would just build sales funnels for him without implementing them because they didn't understand how to apply the appropriate strategy around the sales funnel to address where Dan was at his current position in the market.

Dan brought me in, and I looked at his offers, his sales funnels, and his entire foundation, and discovered where the money holes were. Money holes are where money flows out and is left on the table. Obviously, you want to be able to keep as much of your money inside of your business as much as possible.

After working with me, and over time, Dan has become really proficient at technology, and technology has not prevented him from growing his business. He has either hired it out to the right people, or he has just simply buckled down and learned from the right people in how to apply the tech to his business. But again, his whole goal is not to learn technology and to become a professional marketer. His goal is to get more deals that affect the world with his content and with his message. Once you know who the right people are, you can simply have them implement the tech by hiring either your own team or hiring someone else to do the tech for you. However, you still need the strategy to know when to do things, how to do things, why to do things, and what you should be doing so that you can succeed. You have to know enough to realize that a sales funnel without a strategy is useless

Something specific that you should not do is try to do it all by yourself and try to become a marketer. Your goal is not to become an expert marketer. Your goal is to get more deals, grow your business, and generate more content. Your goal, though, is to learn how marketing is done the right way and either do it yourself, or have someone else do it for you, whether that means you hire a team, or you do something else. You need to learn how things are done online and how tech works so that you can experience real progression in your business and not become stuck.

One thing you can do right now to grow your real estate business, to educate more people to get a quick win, and overcome this roadblock is market research. Post on your social media platforms, or inside of Facebook groups and ask questions. Ask the following question on your profile or inside of groups: "When it comes down to ______, what is the number one thing you struggle with?" By asking similar questions like this, you will get a lot of people to answer your question, and this is where customer research starts. You need to be able to understand what people say and how to create offers based on what people say online. Then, you create content based on the responses you get from your posts. You'll be surprised at how many people you will get to message you to do business with you when you do this correctly. Whether you believe it or not, you can make an extra 6-7 figures per year in your real estate business by posting once per day on your favorite social media channel.

How do you do this correctly? The following strategy is what I like to call the Perfect Posting System, which I also called the 3-2-1 Method back in the day. The following method has produced millions of dollars across the board collectively for all the real estate professionals I've helped.

What you want to start with is a post per day. Every single day you should post on your favorite social media profile. For example, Facebook is where I like to have all my real estate professionals start posting.

What should you post? The Perfect Posting System consists of 3 types of posts: Lifestyle, value, and business. You want to post 3 lifestyle posts in a row daily, 2 value posts in a row daily, and 1 business post after that. Let's talk about each one a little more in depth:

Lifestyle posts are meant to build relationships with your audience. Have you ever noticed some people post the weirdest content on social media? They post weird, grainy photos of the most random things, weird memes that have no context, and they have no theme to their posts. What you should do is post pictures of yourself, your family, special outings, vacations, and regular things that you're doing in your life. When you post lifestyle posts, you will typically get the most likes and comments. When people like and comment with your content, they will more likely see your posts in the future. Here is an example from one of my clients:

Let's now talk about value posts. Value posts are meant to educate your audience. These can include steps, tricks, hacks, tactics, strategies, and tips that will help your audience get a desired result. Value posts are meant to show your expertise without being spammy or desperate. You will gain more respect from your audience by teaching them how to overcome their problems in trying to buy houses, sell houses, or get started in real estate. For example, you may teach sellers how to sell their homes quicker with 3 simple steps. Start off your post by saying, "If you're looking to sell your home, here are 3 things you can do right now to make sure it sells quick." Then you want to list the 3 things and give them advice on how to sell their homes fast and effectively.

Mike Baird
August 4 · 🌐

What if I told you that you could make an extra 6 figures or more per year in your real estate business, without spending a dime on advertising or marketing?

What if I also told you that you could get free leads from Facebook that turned into deals?

A few weeks ago while I was at Lake Powell, I had my marketing expert Tucker, educate our Tribe Members on how to use social media to get deals to CHASE THEM vs them chasing deals.

If you're ready to start establishing your personal brand online, and you want to put yourself out there as a real estate expert, and get your calendar filled with people who want to do business with you, then watch the video in the comments below!

👍❤️ You, Larry Reeves, Chase Scott and 21 others   5 Comments

👍 Like   💬 Comment   ↪ Share

Let's finally talk about business posts. Business posts are meant to get you paid. These types of posts ask for the sale or what I like to call "Micro Commitments." Your goal is to have them take action and get closer to paying you money, doing a business transaction with you, or pay you for your coaching programs. You want to write a post that asks them to download, watch, or buy something. Check out this business post example that lead to actually generating leads and conversations with serious buyers:

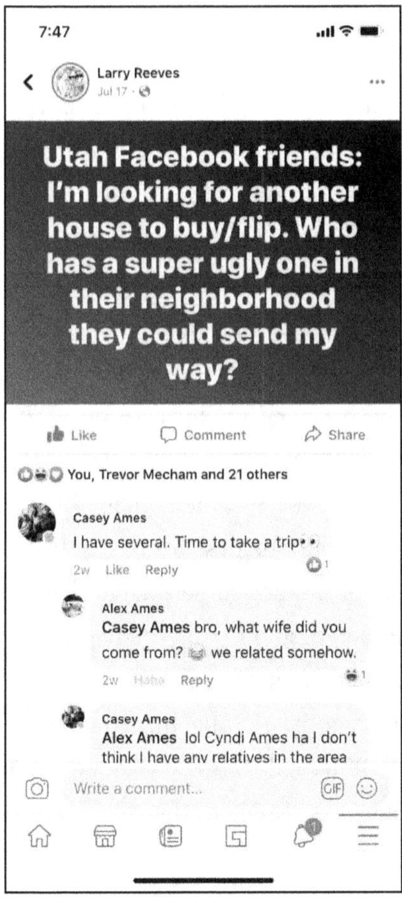

See how easy this is? Most people post the most random things on social media and damage their reputation. They look too spammy when they always post about business, and aren't taken seriously when they only post lifestyle posts. By following this system, you can expect a well-rounded content strategy that will grow your business.

Now I've had people come to me saying they don't want to post about their family, or they don't want to use social media. They also say they don't want to show certain posts to certain people and they don't think that social media works for business because they don't want to post about business to their friends. Some also don't want to post because they're afraid of bugging their friends and family.

I've heard every objection under the sun when it comes to using social media, but to be completely honest, this is where you will have the best and quickest results. There are ways to make it work as long as you follow the strategy. The Perfect Posting System is the best content plan for social media that allows you to grow your business for free online without wasting tens of thousands of dollars on paid advertising or obsolete and outdated marketing methods, or damaging your reputation online. It's the best content plan that allows you to build relationships with people, letting them know who you are and what you're about by educating them on what you do, and growing your business. My question is this: Would you rather have excuses and opinions or would you rather get paid? The steps I have just shown have worked for every real estate professional that has simply applied it. Maria is using the Perfect Posting System and within a few months had made $18,000 in her remodeling business as she becomes a flipper. She's using the Perfect Posting System to grow both of her businesses for free.

Now, let me tell you another story about Stuart and Ben. Stuart and Ben knew about digital marketing, but they didn't know how to start when it came down to growing their business online and growing their real estate company. By understanding the mechanisms of digital marketing and by creating an education business to get more customers and deals, they are now growing their real estate company online. It's a matter of creating and researching what people want and giving them the solutions they need. Continue conducting the customer research methods; do it all the time. You must understand your customers, which will validate your ideas before you turn them into products or coaching programs.

Post on your Facebook profile and send emails to people asking them what they struggle with. Ask them what their fears are. Ask them what their doubts are. Ask them what they struggle with on a regular basis, or when it comes down to a specific topic. By asking these questions and documenting them, documenting them in Google spreadsheets, and then analyzing the data, you will be able to grow your real estate company.

If you're talking to investors, this also works for consumers. You can ask simple questions on your Facebook profile, such as: "When it comes down to buying a house, what is the number one thing that you struggled with?" And you can look at all of the answers and create solutions for people in buying a house. The current education system in the world right now is failing people because they're spending hundreds of thousands of dollars on a college education to get a four-year degree, and it does not pay off. People are turning to experts just like you, who are actually doing what you're teaching regularly, and more and more people are turning to experts in their field and their market to learn precisely what they want to do.

People ask for recommendations on social media all day long on every subject imaginable, from where to find hand sanitizer to what's better, Mac or PC? We can leverage that behavior to get people on board with what we are trying to accomplish by asking for recommendations on social media. People ask for recommendations about things that they are looking to buy. Let's just say a new mom gets on Facebook and asks, what is the best stroller? People will then reply and give her solutions for what the best stroller is. By doing this research, she is now finding the perfect stroller for her baby. What my wife did while she was growing her mommy blog on Pinterest was she simply asked the question, "When it comes down to being a new parent, what are the things that you struggle with the most?" We had over 300 people answer this question in a Facebook group, and we simply created offers and content based on their answers.

Let me tell you about a few companies who are doing precisely what I'm talking about when it comes down to research. Amazon, one of the biggest companies in the world, emails surveys to buyers, and asks about their experience. Amazon, based on these survey answers, adapts their business at a mass scale and pivots their offers accordingly. Every single time you buy something on Amazon, they send you an email saying, "Hey, how was your experience with X and Y company?"

These surveys enable Amazon to keep up to date with current trends and find out what people are struggling with so that they can continue to adapt to their market. This is why Amazon is a massive billion-dollar company; they are listening to their audience. They aren't putting the thoughts into their customers' minds. They are allowing the thoughts of the customer's minds to go into their thoughts, which will then help them adapt and pivot their message to their market and grow their business according to what people are saying and doing online. Facebook is another company who is using a company called Qualtrics to do customer research. Customer research is so vital to big companies these days. It's crucial to pose the right questions to your audience to get feedback that is actionable so that you can grow your real estate company.

You may be uncertain about what to say or where and when to post on social media. Maybe you're unsure about how to conduct a customer research survey, or how to run ads to get specific responses. And you might be thinking you don't have an audience, etc. You can overcome this by using somebody else's audience, use your own social media following, your own email list, or someone else's Facebook group. Use comments on blog posts, or use sites like Quora or Reddit or other websites where people are entering in their common questions and concerns about any number of topics.

Let me tell you a story about how we implemented this for Dan Zitofsky. After I started working with him, within the first product launch, we hit five figures by selling his education and selling his online training. Without fully understanding Dan's audience, I asked them questions to understand where they were and what they wanted to learn. I then looked at their responses and helped him create offers based on what he wanted to do, or based on what his audience wanted to buy from him. After we asked a ton of questions, we were able to get thousands of responses and answers around what they were struggling with and how we could help them the most. I also did a bunch of research online through blog posts and Amazon reviews so that I could figure out what people were saying online. Then I crafted an offer based on what people were *already* talking about and what their *struggles* are. Our first launch produced five-figures.

Now, let me tell you, some people are wary of step-by-step guidance and doubt that it works. You may feel this way because you've tried it before, or you've tried to grow your business with education. But how would it feel if you were able to do it, right? How would you feel if you were able to see progress in your business by doing things the right way? This would feel amazing, and you would feel relief after you did things the correct way, right?

This is how you can be empowered right now to put your doubts to rest. I want you to actually go and ask the question right now on your social media channels, and ask the question, "When it comes down to _____, what is the number-one problem that you struggle with?" I also want you to go check out Amazon book reviews on the specific topic that you're trying to sell, or check out blog posts and check out the comments about what people are saying at the end of blog posts.

By doing these things, you will experience a lot of people who will say, "Hey, I'm struggling with _____." Now, if you don't have the right audience, you might hear crickets, but that's okay. You can go and join 10 to 50 Facebook groups, depending on how serious you are about growing your business, and simply asking the question, "When it comes down to _____, what is the number-one problem or struggle that you face?" I promise you that as you do these things, it will inform your content so that you will see an improvement in your messaging and your marketing, you will produce the right education and information business so that you can continue to grow your real estate company.

Chapter Four: Get Results

One shocking statistic that you will experience after doing your customer research is that once you ask these questions and discover what people are struggling with, you will see that 80% of these people will give you the same thing they need for them to do business with you. Let's just say you get a hundred comments or even a thousand comments on one post. You will find out that when you ask these specific questions out of those hundred, 80 of these people will tell you the same thing in many different ways.

When we did this for Dan, we were able to get thousands of comments telling us exactly the two things that they struggled with the most: raising capital and finding deals. We did the same thing for Ben Fredricks. When you ask these right questions, it lays down the framework for how you need to get more deals, generate more business, and grow your education company for your real estate company.

One thing you can do right now to ensure that you get the right responses is to make sure you ask the right questions to the right people, or you're going to hear crickets. If your target audience is not the audience for your questions, then you are going to hear nothing. Make sure that you are asking these questions to your target audience.

The biggest mistake people make when attempting to grow their business is hiring out in exchange for revenue and not having skin in the game. You won't know what to do or when to do it this way. You need to have some skin in the game and make sure that you and whoever you are working with are working together side-by-side to grow your company.

You need to learn to ask the right questions to the right audiences to generate business. If you hire someone who doesn't know what they're doing, they will not get you the results that you are looking for. As I've mentioned before, Dan has spent tens of thousands of dollars hiring the wrong people. Once we worked together, our first launch produced five figures from his courses and online training.

The Prelaunch Profit Method is not just for creating coaching packages and courses. You can also use these same strategies to generate more deals and get more properties and add them to your portfolio. By leveraging this framework, you will generate more course sales, more leads from paid advertising, and get more speaking and consulting gigs, and as layers are added to its foundations.

Sterling Harris is a real estate investor who is on track to making $300k by the end of this year at the time of writing this book by using our social media marketing methods to get more deals from social media.

Larry Reeves got his first deal from social media and is having people reach out to him weekly to see how they can do business with him.

Maria Barraza is a remodeler who has entered the real estate investment space and by posting simple social media posts—the same ones I describe here in the book--she got two remodeling gigs worth $18,000.

Don't do this alone and get help. Trying to figure all this out by yourself will take you years and you might not ever see the results that you're looking for.

Stuart Fox, another one of my students, has tried to do this by himself, and he simply couldn't do it because he didn't know-how. He would have spent three to five years learning how to do all this stuff to create something. Stuart is built to get more deals and grow his business. He needs someone else to implement the process for him, who knows what they're talking about.

Doing absolutely nothing and expecting a change to magically is insane. If you are trying to do the same thing over and over and expecting different results, it's not going to happen. You, as the business owner, need to change the way you're thinking and adapt your message and your marketing to your market.

Dan Zitofsky was so fed up after working with everybody; he needed help. He needed the right person to not only build the system for him but to actually give him the strategy to produce consistent sales and get more deals on a regular basis.

A common misconception that I hear a lot is people think this new routine takes a lot of time. It's simply not true because you can create a year's worth of content in three days.

One thing that you can start doing to grow your education business is to create content on a regular basis, matching your message to your market. Your audience will get to know, like, and trust you while you educate them on your products and services. You can spend three days creating your content, and then you can redistribute and repurpose this content and splice it up into different formats so that you can post it everywhere. One video can be posted on social media platforms such as LinkedIn, YouTube, Instagram, Facebook, Pinterest, et cetera.

Let me tell you about Peng Joon. Peng Joon is a content king. He is really good at creating one piece of content and redistributing that piece of content and creating more pieces of content from that one piece of content. He'll create tens if not hundreds of videos within a three-day period, and then he'll have enough content to then last the rest of the year. It does not take that long to create content. You just need to know the framework and do your research. You can then use this content for marketing your products and services and generating more business online.

This is the way you can start implementing step two, which is creating offers. You can now create an offer off of the research that you have done, and in order to then sell that, you need to package that together and put it inside of the sales system. Your content can then be your traffic generator as you put that on Google Ads and Facebook Ads, and you can also use this research to create your sales pages, your video sales letters, your copywriting, your ads, your emails, etc.

By doing your research, you'll complete 90% of the work upfront. You will be able to have all of your content done by doing the right research. Once your research is done, you can then craft your offer and plug it inside of a sales system and inside sales funnels, get Google Ads and Facebook Ads and other traffic sources onto that—both paid and organic—and then start scaling your company. Those are the five steps.

We have done this exact thing for all of my clients from start to finish when it comes down to growing their companies online. Take Dan again, for example. We needed to figure out what people were talking about, what they were saying, what they were struggling with. We analyzed the data from the research and found out what people were saying and the top 10 things they wanted. Then, we created content, sales pages, emails, and videos based on the data we'd collected. We packaged that together inside of sales funnels and emails and everywhere else, and got traffic on it from his current audience and then sold it to then produce six figures in his business.

I can set you up right now to influence the outcome that you want by using this little secret for success. What you can do right now is search Google, Facebook groups, Facebook Ads, and

YouTube to see what is already being sold. This is step two in research. You need to find out what your competitors are already selling so that you can package together with your other offers and create better offers.

Some people may want to quit at this point, or they not fully follow my guidance, but a common thing that will happen to those who quit or not fully follow my guidance would be that they will quit because they don't see results right away. People make the mistake of quitting too early and miss out on millions.

Let me tell you about Mike Baird. Mike Baird is a real estate flipper who is well-known in the industry, has had TV channels, was featured on large publications, etc. And within the first 33 days of working with me, he got a $10,000 coaching program signed. I was out to lunch when Mike texted, "Hey, I just signed up a $10,000 coaching gig. Can you call me real quick?"

By conducting customer and competitor research, Mike and I generated more traffic and were able to package something together to then sell a $10,000 coaching package. This isn't just for coaching; consider deals as anything that gets you paid.

It's so important to surround yourself with the right people. My mentors who have helped me achieve my results are Dan Henry, Kimanzi, Jeff, Justin Holland, and Dan Zitofsky, among many others.

Justin is the person who taught me about digital marketing and about being around the right people from the very beginning. Because I was around the right people, I went to events and did the right things. I was able to exponentially grow my business. I highly recommend that you start surrounding yourself with people who are crushing things out, who are building their business, who are doing the right things according to what their market is saying and doing. And while you are doing this, you will be able to crush out your business.

Chapter Five: The Ripple Effect

You have results, knowledge, expertise, stories, information, and a message to share. When you apply all of these things in your business online, you will start to see your business grow with great success. You will be able to influence the lives of hundreds, even hundreds of thousands of people. With you being able to do that, you will create a ripple effect of helping others help themselves.

Another story that illustrates the amazing ripple effect is about my friend, Dan Zitofsky. Dan has people all over the place on social media, commenting and telling him how much they've seen a considerable change after they have implemented this stuff inside of his business. As soon as I started working with him, they knew for a fact that something had changed and that he had begun progressing forward towards the main goal.

The same exact thing has happened for my other client, Ben Fredricks, who has already started creating his education business and generating more deals because he started putting himself out there as the expert in getting people to be interested in working with him.

Some people sabotage their success by quitting too early, and they don't do things in the right order, and they allow fear and doubt to make their decisions.

Sometimes people accidentally or intentionally sabotage their own success. They allow excuses and fear around technology to make them quit. For example, Kara, my wife, is a wonderful, amazing person. She has such an adorable personality, and I love her to death. She took a long time to actually figure out what she wanted to do because all she wanted to do was to be a mom. However, early in our marriage, we were struggling financially, so she did a lot of things. She chose to do photography and personal training. She decided to do everything that she believed would be a good fit for her and her personality. But at the end of the day, she did not fit, simply because it just wasn't her. She just wanted to be a mom.

As soon as we had our firstborn, she listened to a podcast where she could earn an income from home by being a mom blogger. So, she got to work, and she is now a full-time mom because of her blog and Pinterest.

We had all these struggles, but she didn't quit. We worked together, side by side, and were able to figure out what best suited her and how she could actually make money by creating an education business of her own. And now she is able to stay at home without taking her daughter to daycare, while she goes to a dead-end, 9 to 5 job.

Something you should never forget about and that will get you ahead through the difficult times, is that there is a lot of help and that there is a lot of hope and you can do this. I only expect you to get 1% better every single day. It's a complete lifestyle change for this to happen.

The best advice I can possibly give you to have success with this is to not give up. Learn from your mistakes and adapt. Ask as many questions as you can, and learn to adapt to the market. One tactical way for you to apply and implement this advice right now is to ask about a problem. Ask your audience right now what their number-one problem is when it comes down to what you are trying to sell. I make every person I work with pose that question to their audience, to simply get to know them and create offers based around that.

Five steps of the Prelaunch Profit Method:

1. Research. This includes competitor research and customer research. You need to go and find out what your competitors are doing and how they're positioning themselves online, and then you just need to follow suit. You also need to do customer research by asking your customers questions, whether current customers or future customers, on what they struggle with and how you can help them.
2. What you then need to do is start packaging together your offers based on the research that you've done.
3. Plug in these offers to a sales system. This sales system includes sales funnels, email marketing, and chatbots.
4. Once you get the sales system up, you just need to get more eyes on your sales system, which is traffic. You

need to leverage your paid traffic, which comes from Facebook ads and Google ads, and then you need to leverage your organic traffic, which is your entire social media following.

5. You then need to scale your business, create more offers, create more systems, hire out a team, create webinars based on your offers so that you can automate the sales set systems, and hire out a sales team to manage your sales calls.

You would never start to build a house without blueprints, right? You would never invest in property without doing your due diligence, correct? Doing these things are vital to growing any type of company, especially in the real estate world, and see the results that you're looking after. The results that you can expect after applying these steps will affect the lives of thousands, and you will get paid in the process.

When I first started applying the Prelaunch Profit Method, I tried to write and launch a book. I didn't do the research the right way. I didn't look into what my customers wanted. I didn't see what was already being sold or how things were put together as sales systems, and I tried to launch a book. I got *one* single sale, and it was a pity sale from a friend. Since that time, I've made tens of thousands. I've helped other companies make hundreds of thousands of dollars by implementing what is currently working, versus failing with their products and services.

Golden rule: Do your research! By not doing your research, you are going to fail miserably, and your products and services are not going to sell your deal. You're not going to close more deals. You're not going to get more coaching students. You're not going to get more speaking engagements. You're not going to get more leads. You're not going to grow your real estate company online if you do not read, do your research, and adapt to the market.

Frankly, there are a lot of uninformed investors, real estate professionals, and real estate companies who have lost tons of money because they don't do their due diligence, whether it's online or offline.

Dan is making a ton of money through his deals, and the first thing he teaches in his training is research. You need to do your research and make sure that you create a real need people want to see in your business.

Chapter Six: Putting It All Together

Following the guidance in this book might give you an explosion of results very quickly, so quick, in fact, that you might feel overwhelmed at first. Now, this is totally fine, and it's understandable. It might also be feeling amazing, but you might also be overwhelmed, and you might not know what to do next. No worries. I'll tell you about when that happened to my students, Dan, Stuart, and Brandon.

Dan: Within the first two months of getting together all of his foundations, doing the research, finding out who his audience was, and keeping in mind I had never done any type of real estate deal in my life, I was able to craft offers that his audience wanted, even though I personally was not an investor.

Stuart: He saw the magnitude and influence that he could have after doing so many deals in his lifetime, so he wanted to create an education business and actually generate more deals and get more coaching students. But, after he started working with me, he got scared because of the sudden influx of business, all of the people who wanted to work with him. Stuart actually had to take his foot off the gas a little bit so that he could catch up, which is totally fine and understandable because he needed to see how this works.

Brandon: He's learning about the Prelaunch Profit Method, and starting to see the real magnitude that research has with a business. If you do not know how to research, and if you do not know how to understand your market and create offers based on what your market wants, you will struggle to grow your company. One tactical example that you can implement right now to influence your potential outcome and the result that you are looking to get after following my guidance, is asking your audience questions to get the feedback that will inform you about precisely what you need to create for them next. That's it. Once you do these things, you will then be able to plug in that offer, plug those things inside of sales systems and start selling them.

Drop this book and do three things right now!
1. Ask questions on your social media profile.
2. Conduct competitor research by Googling your competitors and finding out what they are posting on social media. Study their ads and notice what their Facebook pages look like.
3. Put together a sales system so that you can start creating your offers, sell more deals, and grow your brand online.

Post on your social media platforms and profiles because you already have a warm audience. Start working with those people who are familiar with you to start growing your business.

You should become familiar with what I call "digital speech." It's just like verbal speech, only knowing how and what to post online to get results that you want.

Create as much content as you can according to what your current audience is struggling with, so you can help them with their problems. They will then be more likely to follow you, ask you questions, and work with you, simply because you are very interested and concerned about their lives, livelihood, and problems. Once they see this, they will be reaching out to you. They will say, "Hey, can you help me with this?" And, you will be able to close them on deals and get more business.

Take the Prelaunch Profit Method to the next level and visit my website, www.digitalrealestateexperts.com. You'll start leveraging education, social media, and digital marketing to generate more leads, close more deals, and grow your business to live the lifestyle that you dream of.

So, go to this site right now. Fill out the information, and if you want to create a six and seven-figure online real estate business, then I will see you on the next page.